Bead
tempted

Bead tempted

Over 100 irresistible
ideas and inspirations
for creative jewelry design

Vigdis Mo Johansen

D&C
David and Charles

A DAVID & CHARLES BOOK

Copyright © J.W. Cappelens Forlag, Oslo 2006
Cappelen Hobby
www.cappelen.no
Originally published in Norway as *Den store smykkeboken*

First published in the UK in 2007 by
David & Charles
David & Charles is an F+W Publications Inc.
company
4700 East Galbraith Road
Cincinnati, OH 45236

A catalogue record for this book is available from
the British Library.

ISBN-13: 978-0-7153-2709-8 paperback
ISBN-10: 0-7153-2709-7 paperback

Printed in China by SNP Leefung
for David & Charles
Brunel House   Newton Abbot   Devon

Visit our website at www.davidandcharles.co.uk

David & Charles books are available from all
good bookshops; alternatively you can contact
our Orderline on 0870 9908222 or write to us at
FREEPOST EX2 110, D&C Direct, Newton Abbot,
TQ12 4ZZ (no stamp required UK only);
US customers call 800-289-0963 and
Canadian customers call 800-840-5220.

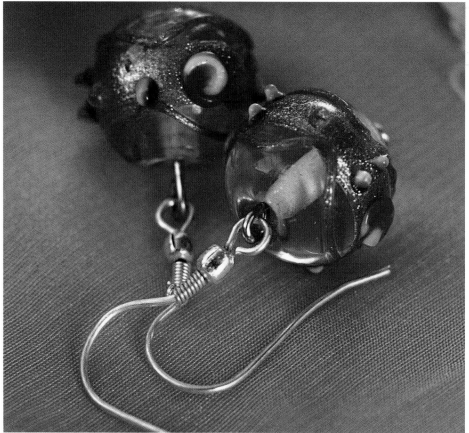

Contents

Preface

This is a book about beads and jewellery, with simple ideas to get your imagination working and inspire you. Here you will find beads in colours that are delicate and romantic or red and intense, while others are in a blue mood. Don't forget that there are lots of beautiful things all around us; the secret is to make the best of these. Shells, strass gems, angels, wool, ribbons and strings of pearls. The challenge is to use your eyes.

Best wishes from Vigdis

I'd like to thank my boyfriend so much for all his help threading beads and other details, also my sons for being patient with their mother, and special thanks go to my suppliers of materials and beads, Idégrossisten and Global Hobby. See page 111 for a range of suppliers.

Tools and Materials

Tools

Good jewellery pliers make light work of the job, so spend a few extra pounds to get some that will last you for years.

- Wire cutters to cut jewellery wire, metal wire, jewellery pins etc.
- Flat nose pliers for flattening rings and jewellery crimps and stoppers.
- Round pliers for bending jewellery pins, metal wire, memory wire etc.

Make sure that the flat pliers have an even inside surface, rather than grooves which will ruin the jewellery crimps. There are also combi-pliers on the market, which combine all the functions. Experiment and find the pliers that suit you best.

Cords

Waxed linen and cotton cords are available in sizes from 0.4mm ($3/16$in) and in a very wide selection of colours. They are used for the popular threaded jewellery pieces that have been on the market for some time, and are as popular as ever.

Metal thread of all kinds and sizes are used for crocheting/knitting of jewellery. For a 0.3mm ($1/8$in) thick metal thread, crochet hook number 3.5 (US size E/4) is best suited.

I always sew on the beads last with the end of the metal thread, whereas others thread all the beads onto the wire before starting off. It is all about finding your own preferred working methods.

Jewellery wire is a slightly spun, thin steel thread with plastic coating. It is incredibly easy to work with, giving the jewellery a professional look. It comes in black, gold and silver, which are the most usable colours, but other colours and shades have been added to the range lately.

Memory wire is spiral wire that comes in three different sizes; necklace, bracelet and ring. Nylon cords, pearl cords and elastic cords are also used for making jewellery. Personally, I am not too fond of elastic cords. In my experience they tend to disintegrate; reducing to history a piece that you might have spent a lot of time and effort on.

Jewellery crimps/stoppers

Small crimp beads come in gold, silver or black. They are threaded on before and after the bead and flattened with flat nose pliers. Use them as a finish before the clasp.

Clamps

There are several kinds of clamps suitable for jewellery. Large ring-locks (12mm / ½in) are excellent for the crocheted bracelets.

Spring hoods with a corresponding eye-ring come in gold, silver and pewter.

Charming heart-shaped and square clasps are well suited to bracelets. Magnetic fasteners are absolutely brilliant, as help is no longer required to put on the jewellery.

A stick clasp is a ring with a stick hooked through it to make a clasp. In addition, there are other clasps so good-looking they are almost jewellery in their own right.

Attaching fasteners

Thread a jewellery clamp onto jewellery wire and then thread the wire through the fastener.

Thread the end of the wire back to the jewellery clamp so that it forms a small loop. Squeeze the jewellery clamp flat using pliers and cut off the end of the wire with pliers or thread the end of the wire into the first bead.

At the end of the job, do the same at the other end of the wire, but here with a bolt ring fastener. Be careful to tighten your work before attaching the fastener.

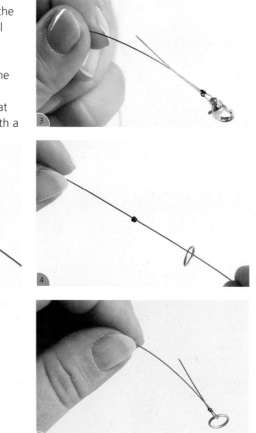

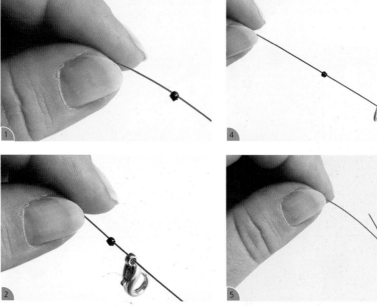

Using headpins

Thread the bead onto the pin and cut off the pin about 1cm ($^3/_8$in) from the bead.

Bend the pin 90 degrees towards the bead, using round pliers.

Move your pliers to the end of the pin and bend it around the pliers to make a closed eye. Finally, straighten with pointed flat pliers.

Metal headpins/eyepins

These pins come in pewter, silver and gold colours. They have a small eye or head in one end that stops the bead. They are much favoured for making earrings, but are for charm bracelets. The pins are also used with rings with eyehooks.

Strings/chains

Chains are sold by the metre (yard). They come in a great many varieties and sizes. The pea chain is a variety well suited to charm bracelets/strings.

A novelty on the market are the bracelet/necklaces that come complete with head-pins. For jewellery made with glass beads or freshwater pearls I would recommend the use of a real silver chain.

Rings

A ring is not just a ring anymore. We have used one with eight eyes to hang beads on using headpins (shown left). Gorgeous beads can be glued on to one end of a divisible ring. Tiny beads can be threaded onto a memory wire ring. For flat-top rings, beads can be glued on or sewn on using metal cords.

Earrings

The easiest way to make pretty earrings is to use a hook with a spiral and a bead threaded on a headpin attached to the hook.

Useful items are silver-coloured creole rings with eyes for threading little beads onto, large round ones and drop-shaped ones. Try shiny, sparkly glass chains/strings for long earrings.

Pendants

There are hearts of all kinds, angels by the dozen, butterflies, frogs, dolphins, stars, shoes and crosses. There are even watches.

Metallic décor

These items are available in antique silver and golden colour finishes. Flat and round decorative basins are used on either side of the beads. Look out for princess tiaras, angel heads and sweet little hearts with captions such as 'Made with love' and 'Just for you'.

Miscellaneous items

Tube clasps are useful for jewellery. These have between two and ten holes and are used for making bracelets with several strings of beads that are placed nicely side-by-side. They are completed with a clasp part with holes before fastening the clasp.

Enamel

There is also a wonderful selection of enamel hearts/beads in small and large sizes. They all have cute little floral motifs, and are available in white, brown, turquoise and red, and various other colours.

Beads

There is so much that can be said about beads that they need a book of their own. A small fairytale revolution has taken place since I made my first piece of jewellery and the first jewellery book was published. We now have hand-made beads, fresh-water pearls, wonderful large wooden beads, white wax beads, millefiori glass beads, beads with dots, stripes, checks and flowers to choose from.

There are beads shaped like a fish, as well as cubes. There are beads/hearts with silver and gold foiling. Magnetic beads in

white and grey are a novelty on the market. I could go on like this forever, but I will give you a small piece of advice: if you plan to put a lot of work and effort into a piece, do shy away from the cheapest lacquered beads, as they will only flake off in time.

Swarowski crystals
These come in beads, drops and hearts, etc, and add an extra sparkle to your design.

Chiffon ribbons
Try using attractive chiffon ribbon in a colour that matches the bead in a simple necklace, or a ribbon as a bow on a bracelet. Velour or silk ribbons are also really elegant.

Carabin hooks
These come in different sizes and are used to decorate hand-bags. They are also really good for attaching beads to your key-ring, to make it easier to find.

A few basic principles
Examine carefully the picture of the piece you would like to make. Experience from my classes tells me that most people take a long time to choose the colours. Red is intense, white is pure and green is soothing. Choose your favourite colour, or pick all the colours of the rainbow. Let the jewellery glue dry for at least 24 hours.

Remember that the clasp adds length to the necklace. Practice makes perfect and you will soon have become your own jewellery designer.

Sea Green Brooch

You need:
Assorted beads
Thin wire, 0.3mm
Brooch pins

I found all these beads in a bag; just look at them –
flowers, leaves, drops and egg-shapes. Cut 50cm
(20in) of wire and sew the beads together in a criss-
cross pattern. Finally, sew a pin on the back.

Romantic Glass Beads

This combination of chunky silver chain and turquoise glass beads is gorgeous. To make this bracelet, first use a pair of cutting pliers to cut the silver chain to fit your wrist. Attach a bolt ring fastener. Thread the beads onto headpins, cut off 1.5cm ($5/8$ in) with pliers and form an eye with round pliers. This is attached to the chain. I put a bead in every second link, but if you want them more often, then go ahead.

Friendship Bracelet

Adjust the length of the silver chain to fit the wrist; attach a bolt ring fastener. I have used beads in beautiful shades of blue, attached closely spaced using silver rings, with two blue stars at the fastener. This makes a great gift either for yourself or for a good friend.

By changing the beads you use in your friendship bracelet you can make it more personal.
In this bracelet I collected lots of gorgeous beads in turquoise and silver to create an extra
special present for a friend.

Turquoise Stones

You need:
Eye hooks
Headpins
4 small square beads
2 turquoise glass beads

Thread the headpin through a small square bead, then through the large glass bead and finally through a small square bead again. Make an eye at the top of the pin with round pliers, thread this into the earwire and squeeze it together with flat pliers.

Turquoise Temptation

You need:
Jewellery wire
Jewellery clamps
1 fastener
10 metal ornaments
5 turquoise beads with gold ornamentation
15 small blue beads
Pewter-coloured metal heart
1 small ring

Cut the jewellery wire to length to fit round the wrist. Remember that the fastener adds 1.5cm (5/8in). Thread on the beads and finish with a bolt ring fastener. Attach the pewter heart to a ring which is then attached to the fastener using jewellery pliers. This bracelet is made with really pretty turquoise glass beads with spacers and a heart made of pewter. Make one in your favourite colour.

Turquoise and Silver Set

You need:

35-40 turquoise lustre beads
Headpins
Small rings
1 fastener
1 large turquoise stone
1 small heart

This elegant set consists of turquoise lustre beads and silver eyepins. Thread a bead onto a pin, cut off 1cm (3/8in) with pliers and bend the end of the pin into an eye. Make 35-40 of these, depending on how long you want the chain to be. Finally, connect them together with small silver rings and finish with a silver clasp. In the front, add a pendant made of a large, turquoise stone with a bead and a small heart – or whatever else you like. To make the earrings, use a bead with two eyes (as for the necklace) and finish with a small heart fastened with small silver rings.

Bracelet with Turquoise Lustre Beads

You need:

Turquoise lustre beads
Metal ornaments: stars, circles, hearts and crosses
Silver-coloured chain
1 fastener
Headpins
Small rings
2 fasteners with 5 holes

To make this airy and elegant bracelet you need turquoise lustre beads, 8mm (5/16in) in diameter and metal pendants with mother-of-pearl appearance. For example, you can use stars, crosses and circles with two attachment eyes. You will also need a silver chain with 4.5mm (3/16in) links, as well as small silver rings to connect the various elements together. For the beads, use silver eyepins. Begin by threading the pin through the bead, cut off 1cm (3/8in) using pliers, then use round pliers to make an eye from the rest of the pin. Connect the pins together with pearls, metal pendants and silver links to form five strings fitting around your wrist. Attach each end of the strings to the two halves of a silver clasp with five holes.

Baroque Bracelet

Attach the cord to the fastener and thread on beads alternately. When the bracelet is long enough, tie the other end of the cord to the other side of the fastener. Do the same with the other strings of beads.

This beautiful fastener was given to me by a colleague. Light blue glass beads alternate with small golden embroidery beads. Something old and something new, but mostly my own idea. You can probably find a similar fastener if you take a look in old jewel boxes or in your local second-hand shop.

Indian Necklace

You need:

Terracotta-coloured suede ribbon
Headpins
Turquoise feathers
Glass beads in terracotta and turquoise
Jewellery coils
Glue
Wire

The necklace is made of terracotta-coloured suede ribbon with glass beads in shades of turquoise threaded on pins. The feathers are bound to the pins using thin wire. These ornaments are attached to coil ends, which are glued to the ends of the suede ribbon. The necklace is also attractive when used as hair jewellery.

Copper Crocheted Bracelet

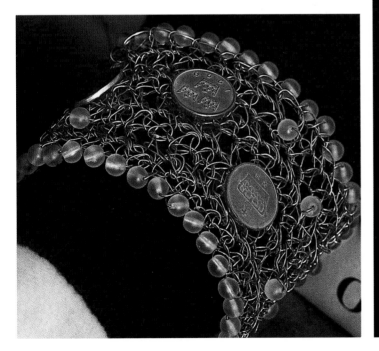

The bracelet is crocheted from 0.5mm copper wire. Turquoise beads are attached along the long edges of the bracelet. You can also attach old coins, to bring good luck, using a glue gun.

Turquoise Tangle

You need:

Wire, 0.3mm
Crochet hook, size 9
Oval metal
ornaments
with angels
Turquoise beads

Crocheted bracelets have been popular for some time, and are still in fashion. Make enough chain stitches to fit your wrist by crocheting back and forth as required, using thin wire (0.3mm) and a size 9 crochet hook (US size M/13). Sew beads into the wire along the outer edges of the bracelet and at the same time attach a bolt ring fastener. The oval angel ornaments are sewn into the crocheted part at the end, evenly spaced around the bracelet. If you would rather knit the wire instead of crocheting it, feel free to do so.

Angels All in a Row

You need:
Oval metal ornament with angel motif
Silver-coloured chain
2 bolt ring fasteners
Small rings
Oblong turquoise beads
Small brown beads
Headpins

The oval angel ornaments also have two holes on each side. Cut 3cm (1 1/8in) lengths of fine chain, which are attached in two rows to the ornaments using small silver rings. Continue until the bracelet is the right size, remembering to take the clasp into account so that the bracelet doesn't get too big. Attach bolt ring fasteners to both chains. Thread turquoise and brown beads onto eyepins and attach them closely spaced along the chains.

Flower Brooch

Use turquoise merino wool and a felting needle. Shape round petals for the flower by sticking the needle in at different angles. Rub the wool with your fingers, turn the flower over and felt it from the other side. Make several petals and felt these onto each other. Continue until you have a flower. Sew in matching beads, and then sew a pin on the back. Alternatively, you can sew on an elastic band or a cord, and make a hair clip or necklace – three things in one.

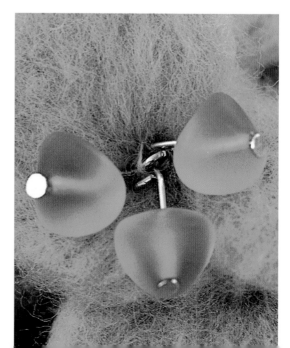

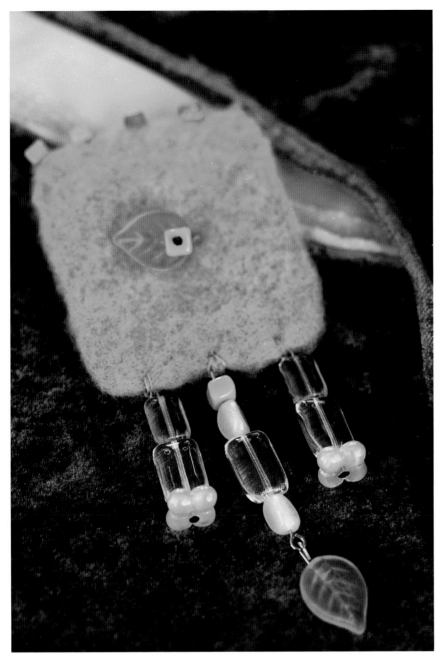

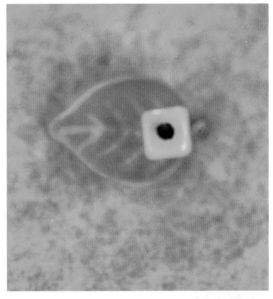

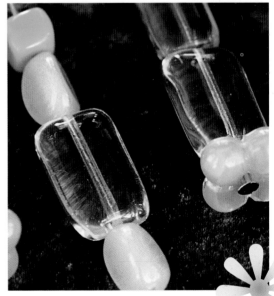

Turquoise Woollen Brooch

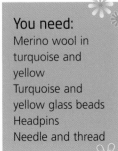

You need:
Merino wool in turquoise and yellow
Turquoise and yellow glass beads
Headpins
Needle and thread

Make a small square of the wool, felt it with the felting needle by piercing the wool over and over. Rub the wool with your fingers, turn the square over and felt it from the other side. Lay a thin twirl of yellow wool over the turquoise wool and felt it in place with the felting needle. Sew on beads as you wish and finally sew a brooch pin on the back.

Long Thread Jewellery

You need:

Waxed linen or cotton thread
Beads of different sizes with holes
of a suitable size for the thread
Metal ornaments

All the thread jewellery uses the same basic method. Calculate how long your chain is to be – from 130-150cm (50-60in) is fine for a long chain. Remember, you must allow extra length for the knots, so the total length should be at least 2 metres (2 yards). Cut the cord at an angle with scissors and apply a little clear nail varnish or glue to harden the end so that it is easier to thread the beads.

Waxed cotton and linen thread can be bought in the shops. The technique is simple: tie a knot, thread on a bead, then tie a new knot. Use coins with holes, buttons, small silk flowers – or anything else you may think suitable.

Fun with Blue

You need:
1 chain with fastener
Headpins
Small turquoise glass beads
Large turquoise glass beads

I make no secret of it – I love blue. Thread large beads onto a headpin, form an eye and attach this to your chain. Here, both the chain and the clasp are pewter coloured. Cool with jeans.

Sweetheart Necklace

The D-ring was meant for a belt, but in this case I want it to lie in the hollow of the neck on a cool piece of jewellery. Thread several strings consisting of jewellery wire and various beads. Fit a clamp on each end with an eye on one end, to which you attach to the D-ring. Turquoise waxed thread is attached at each corner to go round the neck.

Blue Bracelet

You need:
Jewellery wire
Jewellery clamps
1 bolt ring fastener
Round metal ornaments
Sky-blue beads
1 metal star
Glue

You can buy accessories intended to give jewellery an antique look. For this bracelet, use 10mm (³/₈in) diameter round metal spacers with an antique finish.

You will also need sky-blue beads, silver jewellery wire and jewellery clamps. The pendant is star shaped and you can attach a blue bead to it using jewellery glue. The fastener is pewter-coloured to match the spacers.

Turquoise and Pearl Accessories

This jewellery set looks beautiful against sun-tanned skin. To make the ring, cover the square plate on the ring with jewellery glue, then glue the turquoise cross in the middle of the plate. Finally, sprinkle the smallest, brown freshwater pearls all around the cross and let the glue dry thoroughly.

For the necklace and bracelet you need:

Brown freshwater pearls of various sizes
Turquoise glass beads
Turquoise metal pendants in the form of rods, circles and crosses
Pewter-coloured chain
Fasteners
Jewellery wire
Jewellery clamps

To make the bracelet, thread one string of turquoise beads and one string of brown freshwater pearls and turquoise strass stones. Attach the freshwater pearls to the pewter-coloured chain using thin wire. Finally, attach the strings to a clamp. Use a pewter-coloured bolt ring fastener. Attach a turquoise cross to the fastener as a pendant. Make the chain in the same way as the bracelet, but use three different lengths around the neck, so that the chain lies nicely over the chest. Attach two pins and a round, turquoise pendant to the pewter-coloured chain as a central decoration.

For the earrings you need:

Silver earwires
2 turquoise crosses
2 small rings

For the earrings use silver earwires without clasps. Assemble the cross with small silver rings in the earwires. Make sure the side with the turquoise colour faces outwards.

A Special Bracelet

You need:
Oblong silver
fastener with 9
attachment eyes
2 spacers with
9 holes
Jewellery wire
Jewellery clamps
Ice blue beads of
various sizes

The silver clasp in this photo is rather expensive, but it is well worth the money. Take a look at the picture and by all means copy it. I am particularly pleased with this bracelet, and I'm sure you'll be equally pleased with yours.

You can also make a matching ring. Sew beads into a ring using thin wire. Small and large beads make an exciting ring. While you're at it, thread a long necklace using the same beads. This is beautiful on its own, but is really elegant with the bracelet and ring.

Small Pussy Cat

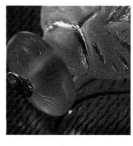

You need:

Earwires
Headpins
2 polished pearls
2 glass beads
2 cat beads

A small bead, the cat bead, and one more small bead, are threaded onto a headpin. Make an eye, which you then attach to the earwire.

Silver Bracelet

Thread silver decorations and beads alternately on the elastic cord. At regular intervals thread on the metal heart, the sandal, the coin, and so on. Take a look at mine, copy it by all means or make one as you fancy.

Long, Ice Blue Necklace

Long, slender necklaces are very stylish and have a distinctive elegance. Cut a length of jewellery wire so that it goes once around the neck. Make sure it is long enough to hang over the chest with the drop-shaped pearl as a pendant in the middle.

Begin by squeezing on a golden clamp. Thread the jewellery wire first through the drop-shaped pearl, then through a round, natural-coloured pearl and then through a round, brown pearl. This is the drop pendant for the front. Now thread lots of small embroidery beads on the wire, with some occasional brown pearls for variation. When the necklace is long enough, thread the wire back through the pendant, the brown pearl, the natural-coloured pearl and finally through the drop-shaped pearl. Finish off with a jewellery clamp.

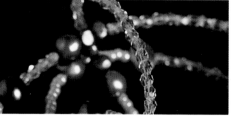

Rainbow Bead Necklace

You need:
Small embroidery beads in a range of colours from pale to dark
White jewellery thread
Jewellery clamps
2 fastener ends with 9 holes
1 fastener

Tiny embroidery beads are excellent for making bracelets with lots of parallel strings. In this bracelet I have used jewellery thread, which results in more flexible strings than stiffer wire would produce. Begin with a silver jewellery clamp, then thread on beads in nine strings, long enough to fit around your wrist. A silver clasp piece with nine holes connects all the strings of beads together. Finish off with a bolt ring fastener.

Pale Blue Drops

You need:
Pale blue beads
Bead holders
Glue
Silver-coloured
chain
1 fastener
Strass flowers
1 coin

Here I have glued pale blue beads to small bead holders using jewellery glue. It's a lot of work, but well worth the effort when you see the result. Attach all the beads to a silver-coloured 7mm (5/16in) chain, two beads in each link. Attach a clasp and hook, fixing a coin and two strass flowers by the clasp.

Elegance in Blue

You need:

Wire, 0.3mm
Crochet hook, size 9
Blue beads in various
shapes and sizes
1 fastener
1 large coin

This bracelet, with its beads in all shades of blue, glitters and sparkles like a clear, starry sky. You'll need thin wire (0.3mm) and a size 9 crochet hook (US size M/13). Crochet chain stitches to a length that fits around your wrist. Crochet plain stitches back and forth to give the required width for the bracelet. Use wire to sew the beads, closely spaced. This may take a while, so be patient. Finally, sew in a ready-made clasp on the short side. Why not add a medallion as a pendant?

Butterfly and Dragonfly Hairgrips

You need:
Small pink beads
Small pale blue beads
Wire
Glue
Hairgrip
Brooch pin
Mesh butterfly, dragonfly or similar

The starting point for these two stylish accessories can be bought ready-made. The butterfly wings for the hairgrip consist of a woven wire mesh. Sew beads closely spaced on the mesh and finally glue to a suitable hairgrip.

For the dragonfly shape, attach beads in the same way as for the butterfly. Then glue a long pin on the bottom and you have an elegant brooch.

Blue Silk Ribbon

You need:
Pale blue Cernit clay
Thin, pale blue
silk ribbon

Roll a cylinder of Cernit clay (or other polymer clay) about 1cm (³/₈in) diameter. Use a sharp knife to cut the cylinder into five thin slices. Press these five petals together to form a flower. Make a hole in each flower before firing. Fire the clay in an oven at 110°C (225°F or gas mark ¼) for 5-10 minutes. Tie the thin silk ribbon to each flower. This flower ornament can be used in bracelets or necklaces.

Velvet Ribbons

Thread cream-coloured pearls of various sizes onto a thin wire. Twist the wires with pearls onto the velvet ribbon and tie a knot in the ribbon to conceal the ends of the wire. Why not make both a necklace and a bracelet? Delicate and romantic.

Lots of Pearls

You need:
1 ring with round mounting plate
Wire
Pearls of various sizes

The rings have a flat plate for mounting ornaments, and can be bought ready-made. Using thin wire, sew on different-sized pearls. Fix the end of the wire to a pearl to finish off. Why not make several to match different outfits?

Summer Favourite

You need:
Silver chain
1 fastener
Headpins
Round pearls in
pastel colours

Cut a length of silver chain to fit the wrist and attach a bolt ring fastener. Pearls in pastel colours, from pale yellow to mint green, are threaded onto eyepins which are attached to the silver chain using pliers. This bracelet is intended to be noticed.

Plaiting with Pearls

You need:
Wire
1 fastener
Round white beads
Some round
coloured pearls

This bracelet uses a simple plaiting technique. Begin by threading four pearls onto the middle of a piece of wire about 1.5 metres (1½ yards) long. Thread on four more pearls and thread the right-hand end of the wire through the second row of pearls. Thread on another four pearls and then thread the end of the wire through the pearls from the left-hand side; then four more pearls and thread the wire from the right. Continue until the bracelet is the required length. Attach a bolt ring fastener.

Chunky Crochet Pearl Bracelet

You need:

Wire, 0.3mm
Crochet hook, size 9 (US size M/13)
Round pearls of various sizes
1 fastener

This pearl bracelet with candy colours is so attractive you could almost eat it up. You'll need thin wire (0.3mm) and a size 9 crochet hook. Crochet chain stitches to a length that fits your wrist. Crochet the stitches back and forth to give the required width for the bracelet. Remember that all these pearls will make the bracelet fairly heavy, so don't make it too wide. Sew on the pearls closely spaced and finish with a strong fastener.

Single String of Pearls

You need:
Jewellery wire
Jewellery clamps
Pearls of uniform size
1 fastener

A simple string of white pearls never goes out of fashion and is as attractive with jeans as with a pretty dress. Use jewellery wire and pearls of uniform size. Attach an attractive bolt ring fastener. Long, short – or both.

Strings of Pearls

You need:
White cotton thread
White pearls
Silver-coloured metal ornaments
Small white shell ornaments

Here I have used white cotton thread. Cut the desired length; I used 2.5 metres (2½ yards). Begin with a knot, thread on a large pearl, then a large knot, tight up against the pearl. Allow a little distance to the next knot, thread on three smaller pearls, then knot again. Continue until you have a pearl and a knot at each end of the thread. Finally, attach a large pearl to finish off. Wind the necklace once or twice around your neck and let the rest hang down.

Pearl Classics

You need:
Jewellery wire
Jewellery clamps
White and cream-coloured pearls
1 fastener
1 fastener end with 3 holes

This bracelet consists of three strings of pearls of the same colour and size. Begin by cutting three equal lengths of silver jewellery wire; squeeze on a silver jewellery clamp about 2cm (¾in) from the end of each wire. Thread pearls closely spaced on each string and finish by squeezing on a jewellery clamp. Remember that the clasp adds to the length, so bear this in mind when you cut the lengths of wire. Use a fastener end with three holes, one for each string of pearls. Finish with a silver bolt ring fastener.

The bracelet with two strings has pearls of various shades, from cream-coloured to golden. You will need gold jewellery wire and clamps. Cut two suitable lengths, thread a jewellery clamp onto each and squeeze it flat. Thread alternating pearls and clamps on both strings. Use the same fastener as for the previous bracelet, only in a golden colour. Attach a large pearl pendant as an ornament at the fastener.

Drop-shaped Pearl Earrings

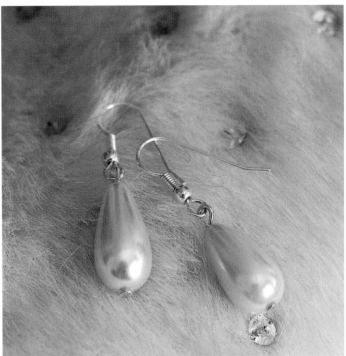

You need:
Headpins
Earwires
2 drop-shaped pearls

Pearl earrings are a classic. To make these, use a silver-coloured headpin, 5cm (2in) long. Thread the drop-shaped pearl onto the silver pin and then cut off 1cm (^{3}/$_8$in) with pliers and bend the remainder of the pin into an eye using round pliers. Finally, add a silver earwire with no clasp.

Pearls and Fur

You need:
Yellow wire, 0.3mm
Crochet hook, size 9 (US size M/13)
Synthetic fur strip
Delicate pink and golden round pearls

Pearls and fur make an exciting combination. To make this bracelet you'll need thin yellow wire (0.3mm) and a size 9 crochet hook. Crochet chain stitches to a length suitable for the wrist and make plain stitches back and forth to the desired width.

When the bracelet is finished, sew on the white fur, which can be bought by the metre (or yard) in craft shops. Sew the fur along the long edges of the bracelet and sew the pearls closely spaced in the fur. Try to find pearls to match the colour of the fur. Finally, sew in two golden fasteners on the short edge of the bracelet.

Pearl Shimmer

You need:

Wire, 0.3mm
Crochet hook, size
9 (US size M/13)
Fastener
Round, clear, white
and grey pearls
and beads

This luxurious, shimmering bracelet speaks of glamour. To make it, you'll need thin wire (0.3mm) and a size 9 crochet hook. Crochet chain stitches to a length suitable for the wrist and make plain stitches back and forth to the desired width. Sew on closely spaced pearls of various sizes. Use pearls in variations from clear to shades of grey. Finish off with a solid fastener.

Mother-of-Pearl Bracelet

You need:

Gold-coloured wire
Crochet hook, size
9 (US size M/13)
Pink and brown
pearls
Strass gems
Gold-coloured star
1 fastener

A pink mother-of-pearl lustre gives a graceful appearance and is always beautiful. To make this bracelet, you'll need thin gold wire (0.3mm) and a size 9 crochet hook. Follow the same crochet instructions as described for the pearl bracelet above. Sew on medium-sized, lustrous pearls in pink and brown shades, as well as strass gems. You can use an antique golden star, for example, as a pendant.

Freshwater Pearl Earrings

I used metal pendants to which I attached earwires. I attached freshwater pearls of varying size to the rings using thin wire.

Summer Party Jewellery

You need:

1 drop-shaped glass pendant with flower motif
Jewellery wire
Jewellery clamps
1 fastener with 5 holes
Pale pink beads
Pale green beads
Round metal ornaments
Glue
Small embroidery beads in pink shades
1 bolt ring fastener
Small rings

The colours of this necklace were chosen to match the colours of the glass pendant – a small pink rose with pretty green leaves. Cut jewellery wire in three equal lengths and attach a jewellery clamp. On two of the strings, thread embroidery beads in shades of pink, and on the third thread clear beads. Finish this off with a jewellery clamp. Now cut a length of wire slightly longer than the others and attach pink glass beads between pairs of jewellery clamps, evenly spaced along the whole length. Squeeze the clamps flat on either side of each pink bead with pliers.

The fifth chain consists of silver spacers, each with two eyes, with a green bead glued to each spacer. These parts are connected together with small silver rings to form a chain. Finally, attach all the strings to a fastener end with five holes. Attach a silver bolt ring fastener. The bracelet is made in the same way as the necklace, but without a pendant.

Hugging the Neck

This unusual necklace uses waxed brown cotton thread and beads in lively colours. See the instructions for the Long Thread Jewellery on page 26.

Gleaming and Golden

You need:
Gold-coloured wire
Golden and brown pearls
1 bolt ring fastener

Brown and cream-coloured beads are threaded onto a thin gold wire. The beads are held in place by making an extra turn around them. Make three strings with the beads in different places. Bind the ends together and attach them to a golden bolt ring fastener.

Radiant Freshwater Pearls

You need:
Grey freshwater pearls
Black jewellery wire
Black jewellery clamps
1 pewter-coloured fastener
1 small, pretty pendant

Thread the pearls and clamps alternately onto the wire. Start and finish with stoppers made by squeezing on jewellery clamps. Use a pewter-coloured fastener and ring. If you would like to have a small pendant, as in the photo, you can probably find something old in your jewellery box which will come into its own again.

Angel's Kisses

This metal square has two holes on each side, making it very easy to use in a ring. Use thin wire and freshwater pearls threaded together. Remember to insert the end of the wire into a pearl, so that it doesn't prick the wearer.

Bronze Brilliance

You need:
Brown embroidery beads
Brown facetted glass beads
Jewellery wire
Jewellery clamps
1 small silver ring
1 heart with angel motif

Small brown embroidery beads and faceted glass beads are threaded closely spaced on a long wire. A heart with an angel motif is attached with a silver ring in the middle of the chain.

Small and Golden

You need:
Rings with
mounting plates
Glue
Small golden beads
Metal ornaments

You can buy silver rings with oval, square or circular mounting plates. Cover the surface with jewellery glue and sprinkle on gold beads, embroidery beads or glass beads. Decorate with strass gems, pearls or jewellery items. Use your imagination . . .

Multilayered Crystal and Silver

Necklaces in different lengths are sumptuous and rakish. You can use clear or matt pink glass beads combined with strass rings and silver rings. Thread two matt pink beads onto an eyepin and make an eye at the other end. Join them together with silver rings, equally spaced, until you have a necklace of the required length.

Thread two strings of clear pink beads, slightly longer than the other, so that they lie nicely in the hollow of the neck. Use the same procedure as for the first strings, except that you make a string of silver rings and two matt pink beads on pins; this string hangs down to the chest. Finish off with a clear glass heart.

The crucifix pendant is made of thin wire and the same beads as in the chain. Begin the cross at the bottom: Bend the wire double and thread on a bead in the middle. Thread the doubled wire up through the beads until you reach what is to be the mid-point of the cross. Divide the wires and push one through the beads and the strass gem. Bend the wire around the last bead and thread it back through the same beads. Do the same with the other wire, and you have made the two arms of the cross. Continue to push the two wires upwards through the beads. Bend the wires into a loop, attach a silver ring, and the cross is finished.

Make the cross in other colours or strass, thread it onto a leather cord which is wrapped twice round the neck, and you have the

Rose Tinted

You need:
1 pewter heart
Pewter-coloured chain
1 bar fastener
Pearls in shades of pink
Pink shell squares
Headpins
Rings

Thread all the beads onto headpins, make an eye on each and attach them one by one to the chain. Attach the shells to rings, which are then attached to the chain using jeweller's pliers. Attach the pewter heart to the front of the chain using a ring. Attach the bar fastener using rings. If you think there are too many beads, just use the pewter heart and the fastener.

Pretty in Pink

You need:
Earwires
Headpins
Pink glass beads
with flower motif

These pretty earrings are made of a large bead threaded onto a headpin. Make an eye to attach to the earwire.

Rose Quartz Bracelet

You need:
Memory wire
Rose quartz
Metal spacers
Small embroidery beads in silver and pale pink
Jewellery thread
Jewellery clamps
Fastener
2 fastener ends with 5 holes
1 metal heart with hole

It's the rose quartz, an irregularly shaped semi-precious gem, that makes these bracelets exciting and out of the ordinary. For one of them you will need three coils of memory wire. Make an eye with round pliers and thread on beads of rose quartz and spacers of metal in random order. This bracelet is heavy, so don't use more than 3-4 coils of memory wire.

To make the other bracelet which consists of five separate lengths, thread embroidery beads in shades of pink onto four different lengths of jewellery wire. Thread a silver heart onto one of the strings of beads for special effect. The fifth string consists of rose quartz stones. Finally, attach all the strings to a clasp end with five holes and add a silver fastener.

Effortless Elegance

This wire can be bought by the metre and is brilliant for those who don't know how to crochet – or who need a piece of jewellery in a hurry! Cut off the required length and attach two small fasteners.

Star, Butterflies and Shells

Silver chain
1 fastener
Pink shell
ornaments
Butterfly
ornaments
1 star ornament
Silver rings

Cut a length of plain silver chain to fit the wrist and attach a bolt ring fastener. Attach the shells to the chain using two silver rings. Attach the butterflies and the star in the same way.

Tipsy Heart

You need:
Jewellery wire
Jewellery clamp
Metal ornaments
1 fastener
Pink and grey beads
1 tipsy heart

Double strings of beads in shades of pink are delicate and romantic. For this bracelet you will need two equal lengths of silver jewellery wire. Begin by squeezing on a jewellery clamp, then thread pink and grey glass beads tightly onto one of the lengths of wire. Finish off with a silver jewellery clamp. On the other length of wire, thread alternating groups of five beads and one pewter-coloured jewellery piece until the length is the same as the string of beads. Attach the end to a clamp before fitting a pewter-coloured jewellery fastener. If you like you can finish off with a heart pendant, a star, a crucifix or a sun.

Cerise Charm Bracelet

You need:
Silver chain
1 fastener
Rings
Metal ornaments
with cerise inlay

This stylish bracelet consists of bars, flowers and round pendants in silver-coloured metal with pink inlay. The pendants are attached to a 4mm (³/₁₆in) silver-coloured chain using small silver rings. The chain can be bought in craft shops by the metre or yard. The bracelet is fitted with a silver fastener. Quick and simple, but stylish!

Throw of Six

How about a little bracelet for luck? Thread equal-sized glass beads, alternating with small embroidery pearls, onto jewellery wire. Press on jewellery clamps on both ends. Attach a bolt ring fastener. Attach lucky charms to the ring next to the fastener: an elephant, a heart, a butterfly with a pink ribbon and a die.

Pink Set

You need:
Round pink pearls
Headpins
Earwires
1 ring with 8 attachment eyes

Plain pink pearls are threaded onto headpins which are cut and attached to an earwire. The earrings are accompanied by a real eye-catcher of a ring. The ring has eight fastening eyes. Thread the pearls onto headpins, cut off 1.5cm (5/8in) and form an eye with round pliers. Attach the eye to the ring and press tight with flat pliers.

Instant Jewellery

You need:
Pink leather cord
White wooden beads
Pink glass beads

Here, pink leather cord, white wooden beads and pink glass beads have come together to form knotted jewellery. The technique is simple: first a knot, then a bead, then a knot, and so on. The length is up to you to decide. This can be used both as a hat band and a bracelet.

Vibrant Charm Bracelet

You need:

White pearls
Pink pearls
Heart with flower motif
Green and pink shell hearts
Clear glass beads
Small green and clear embroidery beads
Headpins
Rings
Chain
1 fastener

Buy a chain that fits your wrist and attach a fastener, or you can buy a chain complete with fastener. Find all the glass beads, lustre beads and hearts you want to use. Thread the beads onto headpins, cut off 1.5cm (5/8in) and form an eye at the end. Attach the beads, three at a time, to small rings, which are then attached to the chain in a pattern.

Shabby Chic

Tear thin strips of cotton material. Thread different-sized pearls onto thin wire. Bind these to a cloth strip and tie knots over the ends of the wires. Wind around your neck or wrist.

Pink Flower

You need:
Pink Cernit clay
Thin, pink silk
ribbon

The procedure for making this pretty necklace is the same as for the Blue Silk Ribbon necklace on page 42, but the size is slightly larger. Attach a silk ribbon with the same delicate pink colour or make a complete contrast by using a rough leather cord. Cernit polymer clay is a material that's fun to work with.

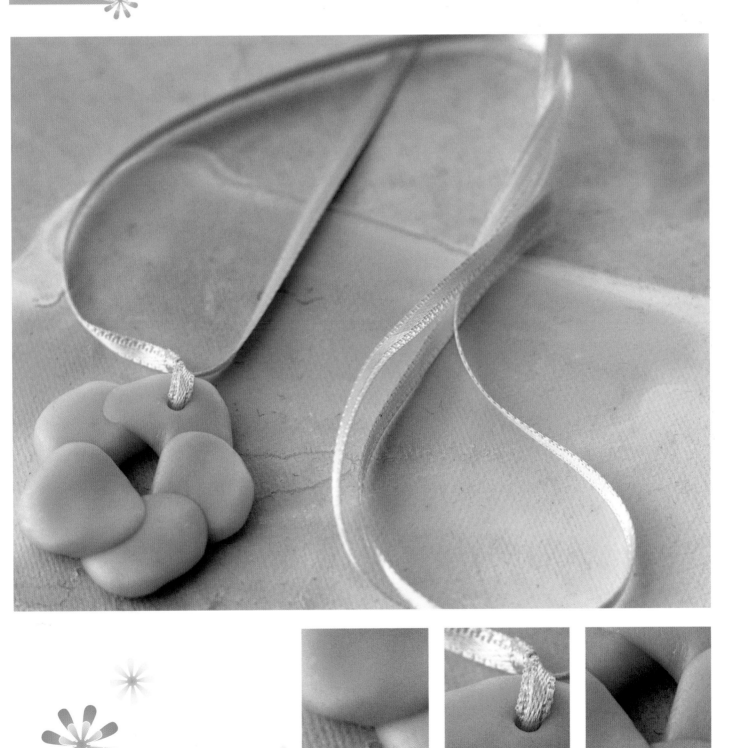

Spiralling Pink Hearts

Memory wire is a fantastic invention. Using these coils as a starting point you can create trendy jewellery in no time! To make this bracelet, start by making an eye on the coil using round pliers. Then thread on beads of various shapes and colours. Don't be afraid to alternate pale pink with orange or red – this makes the design more striking. When you have filled all ten spiral rings with beads, finish off by making an eye at the end using round pliers. Make a bracelet for each of your outfits.

Pink for Everyone

Girls of all ages adore pink. This bracelet uses metal spacers that can be bought in round, oval and square shapes with decorative stones in different colours. The spacers have an eye on each side, making it easy to fasten them together to make small silver rings. When you have the length you want, finish off with a silver fastener.

Tom Thumb

This bracelet is made
using a watch strap,
perforated with a hole
punch, with a row of
beads attached using
headpins. A new trend!

Pink Spikes

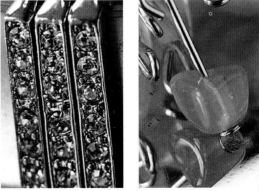
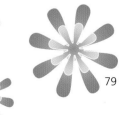

You need:
1 watch strap
Headpins
Clear, white and pink pearls
1 yellow heart
Hole punch

This bracelet was really fun to make. The strap is from an old watch. I made lots of holes with a punch. Where the clock mechanism used to be I attached strass gems from an old, long-forgotten piece of jewellery. Thread a headpin through a hole in the strap, add pink beads, cut off 1.5cm (5/8in) and make an eye with pliers. Continue until the whole strap is full of beads. A bit odd, but fun!

Eye-Catcher

You need:
Wire
Small embroidery beads
5 large beads

This ring is made of small embroidery beads, using a simple plaiting technique. Thread five beads onto the middle of a piece of wire about 30cm (12in) long. Thread on five more beads, take the end of the wire in your right hand and thread it through the second row of beads. Add another five beads and then thread the end of the wire in your left hand through the third row of beads. Continue until the bracelet is of the required size. Sew the ends together and finally sew larger beads to the front of the ring.

Plaited Bracelet

You need:
Wire
2 bolt ring fasteners
Pink pearls of
uniform size
Headpins
1 small heart
4-5 large pink beads

This bracelet is made in the same way as the Eye-Catcher ring opposite. Start with 1.5 metres (1½ yards) of wire, and if you find that's not enough, it's easy to add some more. Until you are familiar with the technique, it's best to use beads of uniform size. Attach two small bolt ring fasteners. For additional decoration you can add some slightly larger beads and some pretty little hearts.

Pink Butterflies

Cut a chunky silver chain to the required length using pliers. Attach a bolt ring fastener. Attach the beads to headpins and bend the ends to make eyes, which then are attached to the chain. What 'makes' this bracelet is different shades of pink and lots of beads. Attach two butterflies by the fastener.

Shades of Purple

You need:
Natural-coloured
waxed cotton thread
Purple beads

Use natural-coloured waxed cotton thread, about 2.5 metres (2½ yards) long – and get knotting! See the instructions for the Long Thread Jewellery on page 26.

Purple Simplicity

You need:
Jewellery wire
Jewellery clamps
1 fastener
Small embroidery
beads
Round and square
purple beads

Cut the required length of jewellery wire and press on a jewellery clamp with flat pliers. Thread on three matching beads and press on a clamp close to the beads. Leave a little space to the next clamp, then add beads and a new stopper. Continue until you have beads all the way round the wire.

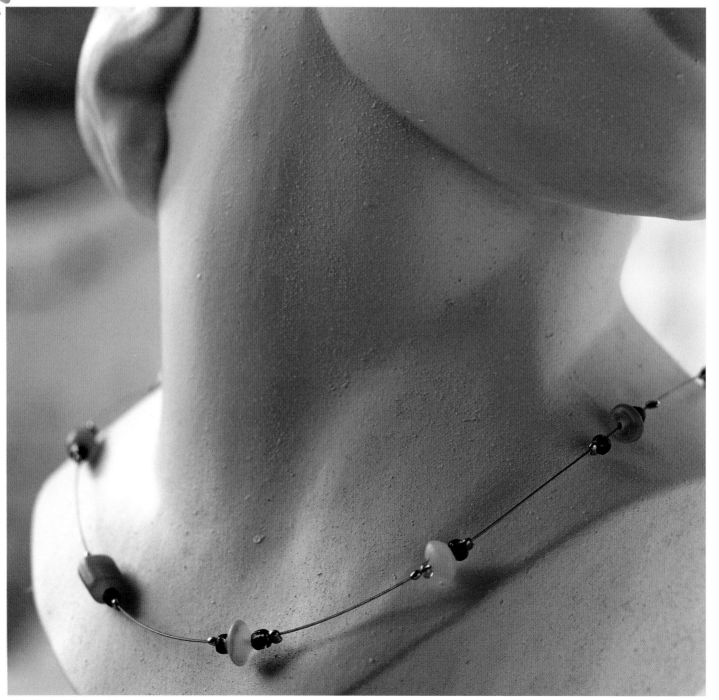

Purple Perfection

Cut three lengths of wire to fit around your wrist. Press on a jewellery clamp, thread small beads onto two of the strings and slightly larger ones onto the third. Fasten all three strings to a ring at one end and to a fastener at the other. Thread beads onto headpins and make eyes at the ends of them, then attach them by the fastener for decoration.

India

All these beads come from the same set from India. The method is as before, but the pearls make these earrings unique. First thread a small pearl, followed by a large one and another small one, onto a headpin. Make an eye with round pliers and attach this to the earwire. Ready for a new pair!

Flower Clasp

You need:
1 fastener with flower motif
Chain
Headpins
Silver beads
Clear and white beads
1 angel
1 heart

The thing to accentuate on this bracelet is the fastener. Cut the desired length of 5mm (3/16 in) silver chain. Attach the fastener with a ring to each end of the chain. Thread clear and silver-coloured beads onto a headpin, form an eye and attach this to your chain. I added a heart and a small metal decoration with angel motif, but this is optional.

Faith, Hope and Charity

You need:
1 cross
1 angel
1 oval metal ornament with lion motif
1 brooch pin with 3 attachment eyes

This pin has three rings for attaching pendants. Many different patterns of pendants are available in the shops. Choose ones that suit you. The pin is suitable for a lapel or as a decoration for a scarf or handbag.

Pewter Hearts

The bracelet is made of silver-coloured, 7mm (5/16in) chain. Cut a length to fit your wrist, using pliers. Remember that the fastener adds to the length, so don't cut it too long. Attach the hearts to the chain at regular intervals with rings. Notice the fastener – this is a piece of jewellery in its own right.

Elegance in White and Silver

You need:
Silver metal parts with
2 attachment eyes
Silver rings
1 fastener

Seven silver-coloured spacers each
with two attachment eyes are
assembled with silver rings between
them. Finally, attach a fastener and
a ring at the ends. A classic bracelet
that you will enjoy wearing for
many a year.

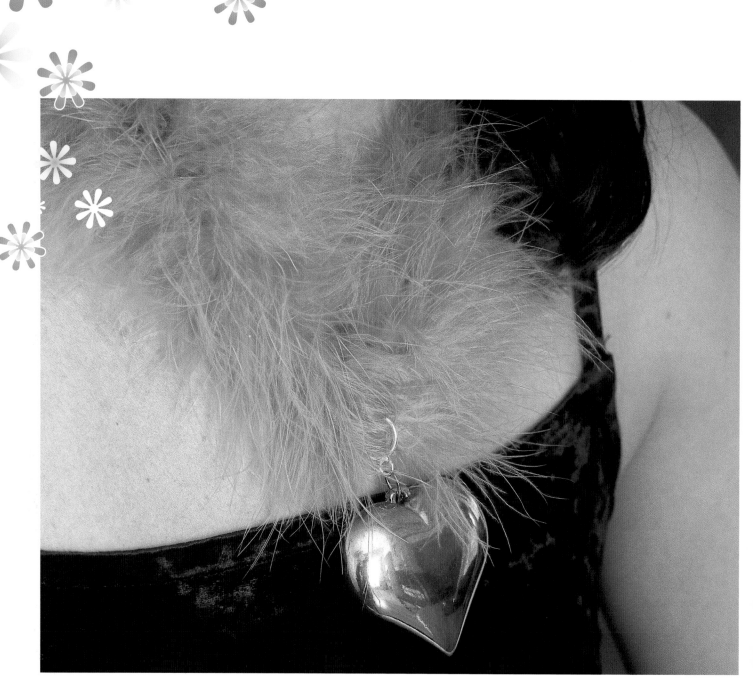

Boa Chain

There are lots of belts and chains for jewellery designers to express themselves with. Miniature feather boas can be bought in different colours and give a glamorous appearance to even the plainest outfit. Cut to length to go round your neck, thread on a large heart pendant or similar – find something in your box of 1980s costume jewellery, for example – and sew a large bolt ring fastener to the ends of the boa.

Free Fantasy

This pin is larger than the one on page 89 and has no rings for attaching ornaments, so use thin jewellery wire and rings threaded onto the pin. Use any odds and ends you have lying around. Mine has buttons and different coins given to me by friends. A very personal pin.

Strass Pin

You need:

Thin wire
1 small adjustable ring
Clear, leaf-shaped beads
Small silver beads
1 brooch pin

This was originally an adjustable strass ring that I adapted. Bend out the ends with flat pliers, and you have two areas to work with. Thread thin wire with leaf-like beads, with small silver beads at the outside edges. Sew all the way round the flower, and then sew a pin on the back.

The Little Black One

This pewter chain with fastener has black beads from a set from India. Thread the beads onto a headpin, form an eye with round pliers and attach this to your chain. Continue to add beads until you feel the bracelet is finished.

Romantic White Roses

You need:
Silk flowers
Silk ribbon
Needle and thread
Fasteners
1 ring with mounting plate
Glue

Silk flowers make beautiful decorations on jewellery. To make a simple choker, sew a silk rose to a thin silk ribbon and attach two small fasteners at the back of the neck.

The ring has a flat surface 2cm (¾in) in diameter and the rose is attached with jewellery glue. The metal hairgrip is 9.5cm (3¾in) long and also has a white silk rose glued to it, using a glue gun.

Sumptuous Silk Flower Set

You need:
Memory wire for neck, arm and finger
Small lime-coloured, white and purple embroidery beads
Silk orchids
1 silver ring

To make this glamorous jewellery set you need coils of memory wire and small beads of various colours. The wire is thin, just 0.8mm, so even the smallest beads can easily be threaded on. Wire coils can be bought in sizes suitable for necklaces, bracelets and rings. Use two wire coils for the necklace and four for the ring. For the bracelet you can easily use ten coils. The more the better! Thread on small beads in the desired colours. Attach the silk orchids with silver hooks; the flower colours decide what colours you choose for the beads – white, olive, purple. Start and finish the wire by bending it into a small ring.

One Ring or Two

You need:
Glue
Strass beads
Small embroidery beads
Rings with mounting plates

Making rings is great fun. Ready-made rings to be decorated can be bought at hobby shops in many shapes and sizes. The width of the ring with strass gems is 6mm (¼in). The stone and heart are attached using jewellery glue. The silver ring with embroidery beads has a plate 18mm (¾in) square. Cover the entire square plate with glue, sprinkle on embroidery beads and add a strass gem in the middle. Remember to make sure the glue is dry before you go to a party!

Crochet Silver Bracelet

You need:
Wire, 0.3mm
Crochet hook, size 9
Clear glass atlas beads
2 large fasteners

The same starting point provides many possibilities for making jewellery. Use a size 9 crochet hook (US size M/13). From a crocheted wire bracelet you can make many different bracelets by attaching beads in different places: along the long edges, tightly spaced or more thinly spread. Finally, sew on a large silver fastener.

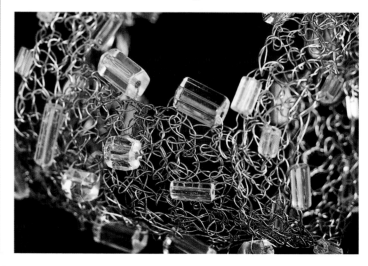

My Favourites with Jeans

This bracelet and ring can be crocheted as described on page 22. Use black wire. Attach colourful facetted beads along the long edges of the bracelet. You will need beads of two different sizes – small ones for the ring and larger ones for the bracelet.

Ice Blue Heart

Ice blue heart-shaped beads are fastened to a chunky silver chain using headpins. Attach a bolt ring fastener. Attach silver decorations in the form of keys, stars or similar at regular intervals. Very delicate.

Lively Hearts

You need:
Red merino wool
Felting needle
Needle and red thread
1 brooch pin
Headpins
Pink, red and green beads
1 round metal ornament with 8 attachment eyes
Small red embroidery beads

The heart is one of the best-known and dearest symbols. This red heart forms a pin and is made of merino wool worked with a felting needle. When the shape is the way you like, long and narrow or broad and rounded, sew on beads where you want them. Finally, sew a pin on the back of the heart.

An Explosion of Colours

You need:
Multicoloured beads of uniform size
Silver wire
Crochet hook, size 9

This colourful bracelet is made from silver wire and facetted beads. Look at the instructions for the bracelet on page 22. Use a size 9 crochet hook (US size M/13). Sew on the beads closely spaced and don't be afraid of mixing colours. The beads are intended for children, as the bright colours suggest.

Red Thread Jewellery

You need:
Red waxed cotton thread
Pink beads
Orange beads
Red beads

Look what different textures and effects the beads produce! Here we have red cotton thread and beads in pink, red and orange. Intense! See the instructions for Long Thread Jewellery on page 26.

Rosy Red Collection

You need:
Red beads with flower motif
Green beads
Small red embroidery beads
Headpins
1 ring with 8 attachment eyes
Earwires

All these beads come from a box of assorted beads in different sizes and patterns. It's the beads that 'make' the earrings. The ring is really attractive. The ring shape has eight small attachment eyes. Thread the beads onto an eyepin, cut off 1.5cm (5/8in) with pliers and form an eye with round pliers to attach to the eyes on the ring. Small beads are particularly effective.

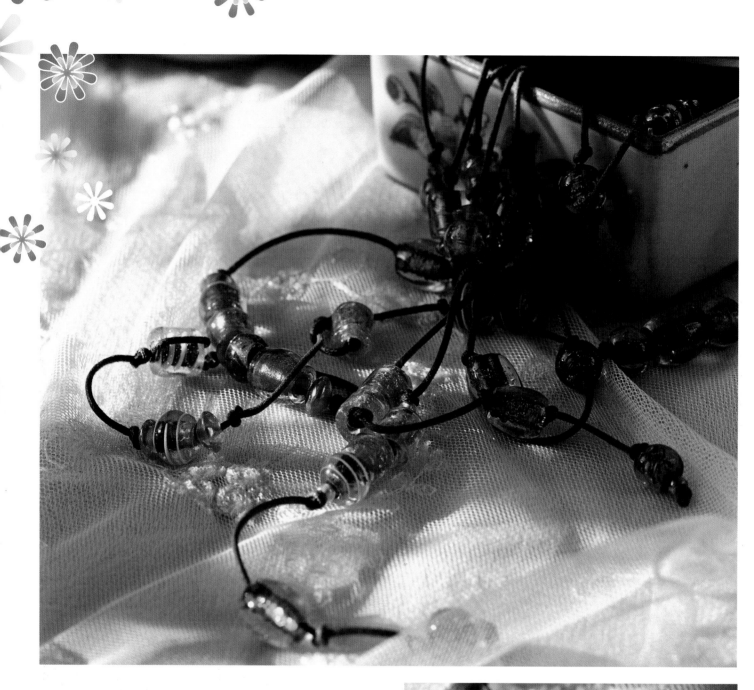

Candy Colours

You need:
Waxed blue denim cotton thread
Candy-coloured beads

Waxed blue denim thread and a mix of beads in colours that get noticed. Knot, bead, knot – simple and pretty.

Is the hole in the bead too large?
Take a look at this photo to see what I did!

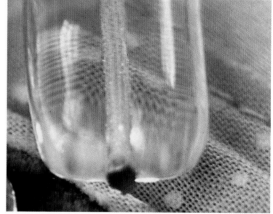

Instant Sunshine

You need:
Yellow beads
Earwires
Headpins

These earrings look good against tanned skin. Thread a headpin through the bead, make an eye with round pliers and attach this to the earwire.

Cute as a Button

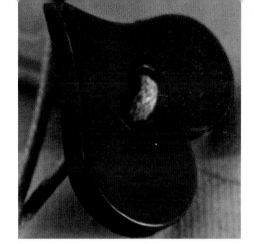

These red hearts are buttons. Thread waxed cotton thread in the button holes with a little distance between them, and make a knot at each end of the thread. Finished! A quick bracelet that is easy to make, fine for a first date or Valentine's Day. Have a look in the shops; there are buttons with many different motifs.

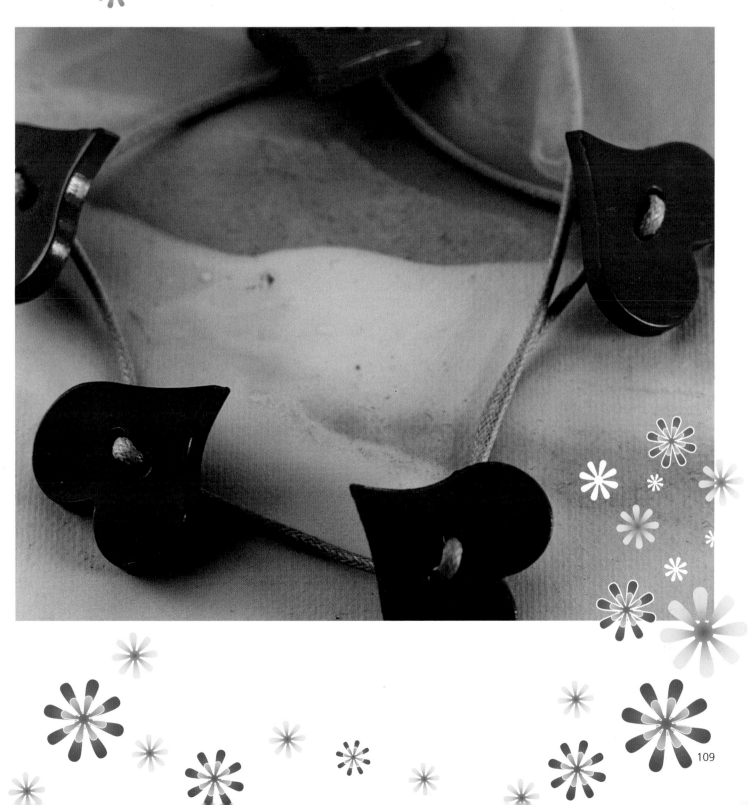

Chic Shells

You need:
Ornamental ribbon
Knitting needles, size 11 (US size 0)
Needle and thread
White pearls
Round white shells
Small embroidery beads
Natural-coloured waxed cotton thread

Here I have knitted with ornamental ribbon and size 11 knitting needles. Cast on seven stitches and knit plain stitch back and forth until the pendant is of the desired length. Then use a needle and thread to sew on shells with small embroidery beads and glass beads until it is completely covered. Thread waxed cotton thread into the end of the pendant, and make a knot to fasten it. This piece of jewellery can be worn in the hollow of the neck or on the chest, depending on where you tie the knot.

Suppliers

UK and Europe

The Bead Shop
104 – 106 Upper Parliament Street, Nottingham NG1 6LF
tel: 0115 9588899
email: info@mailorder-beads.co.uk
www.mailorder-beads.co.uk

Claire's Accessories
(Worldwide chain throughout Europe and USA)
For your nearest store:
email: customerservice@claires.com
www.claires.co.uk

Constellation Beads
PO Box 88, Richmond , North Yorkshire DL10 4FT
tel: 01748 826552
fax: 01748 826552
email: info@constellationbeads.co.uk
www.constellationbeads.co.uk

Creative Beadcraft
20 Beak Street, London W1R 3HA
tel: 0207 629 9964
tel (mail order): 01494 778818
email: beads@creativebeadcraft.co.uk
www.creativebeadcraft.co.uk

Hobbycraft Superstores
Stores throughout the UK
Help Desk, The Peel Centre, St Ann Way,
Gloucester, Gloucestershire GL1 5SF
tel (for nearest store): 0800 027 2387
tel (mail order): 01202 596100
www.hobbycraft.co.uk

Josy Rose
PO Box 44204, London E3 3XB
tel: 0845 450 1212
email: info@josyrose.com
www.josyrose.com

Kleins
5 Noel Street, London W1F 8GD
tel: 0207 437 6162
email: mail@kleins.co.uk
www.kleins.co.uk

Knorr Prandell and Gütermann
Perivale-Gütermann Ltd, Bullsbrook Road, Middlesex UB4 OJR
tel: 0208 8589 1624
www.gutermann.com

The London Bead Company
339 Kentish town Road, London NW5 2TJ
tel: 0870 203 2323
email: londonbead@dial.pipex.com
www.londonbeadco.co.uk

The Spellbound Bead Company
45 Tamworth Street, Lichfield Staffordshire WS13 6JW
tel: 01543 417650
www.spellboundbead.co.uk

The Viking Loom
22 High Petergate, York Y01 7EH
tel: 01904 765599
email: vikingloom@vikingloom.co.uk
www.vikingloom.co.uk

Tout à Loisirs
50 Rue des Archives, Paris 75004, France
tel: 01 48 87 08 87

V V Rouleaux
54 Sloane Square, London SW1W 8AX
tel: 0207 730 3125
email: general@vvrouleaux.com
www.vvrouleaux.com

USA

Joann Stores, Inc
5555 Darrow Road, Hudson Ohio
tel: 1 888 739 4120
email: guest service@jo-annstores.com
www.joann.com

M & J Buttons
1000 Sixth Avenue, New York, NY 10018
tel: 212 391 6200
www.mjtrim.com

Mill Hill, a division of Wichelt Imports Inc.
N162 Hwy 35
Stoddard WI 54658
tel: 608 788 4600
fax: 608 788 6040
email: millhill@millhill.com
www.millhill.com

Index